Learn ASP.NET MVC

Be ready for coding away next week using ASP.NET MVC 5 and Visual Studio 2015

Arnaud Weil

Learn ASP.NET MVC

Be ready for coding away next week using ASP.NET MVC 5 and Visual Studio 2015

Arnaud Weil

This book is for sale at http://leanpub.com/aspnetmvc

This version was published on 2016-01-08

ISBN 978-1-326-48303-6

To my wonderful wife and kids. Your love and support fueled this book.

Contents

Introduction

What this book is not

I made my best to keep this book small, so that you can learn ASP.NET MVC quickly without getting lost in petty details. If you're looking for a reference book where you'll find answers to all the questions you may have within the next 4 years of your ASP.NET MVC practice, you'll find other heavy books for that.

My purpose is to swiftly provide you with the tools you need to code your first ASP.NET MVC application and be able to look for more by yourself when needed. While some authors seems to pride themselves in having the thickest book, in this series I'm glad I achieved the thinnest possible book for my purpose. Though I tried my best to keep all of what seems necessary, based on my 14 years experience of teaching .NET.

I assume that you know what ASP.NET MVC is and when to use it. In case you don't, read the *What is ASP.MVC* chapter at the end of this book.

Prerequisites

In order for this book to meet its goals, you must :

- Have basic experience creating applications with .NET and C#
- Have working knowledge of HTML
- Know what a Web application is

How to read this book

This book's aim is to make you productive as quickly as possible. For this we'll use some theory, several demonstrations, plus exercises. Exercises appear like the following:

 Do it yourself: Time to grab your keyboard and code away to meet the given objectives.

Tools you need

The only tool you'll need to work through that book is Visual Studio 2015. You can get any of those editions:

- Visual Studio 2015 Community (free)
- Visual Studio 2015 Professional

Source code

All of the source code for the demos and do-it-yourself solutions is available at https://bitbucket.org/epobb/aspnetmvc

1. Creating our Web Site

Here's how we create an ASP.NET MVC Application.

Remember: you watch and memorize this, don't try to do it now. Please bear with me, I promise you'll get fun a bit later.

Let's start Visual Studio 2015 and select File / New / Project from the menu. I know New Web Site sounds tempting but don't use it, that kind of site doesn't scale up well once you get to real applications.

I'm taken to the New project dialog box:

From the left menu I'll select Visual C# since it's the most common coding language for .NET, then Web. In the middle pane I'll select ASP.NET Web Application and in the right pane I'll ensure the Add application Insights to Project is unselected (because I don't need them). In the lower part of the dialog box I'll type the name of my project: Demos.

Now I click the OK button and I'm taken to a second dialog: New ASP.NET Project. Time to select the features we want. I'll select MVC and keep the other default options as shown on that screenshot:

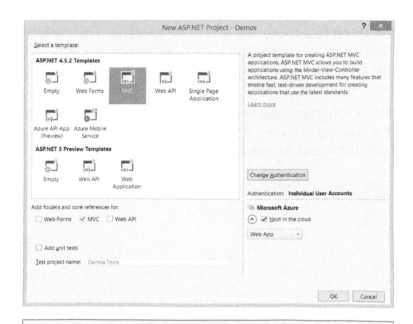

Just a word on the other options, in case you wonder. Add unit test can be unchecked, because it's
easy to add unit testing later on when we need it.
Host in the cloud is checked and Web app is se-
lected since this will provide me an easy-to-deploy
free hosting from Microsoft Azure. And having the
Authentication: Individual User Accounts ensures
that it's dead-easy to get a local database (or SQL
Server with one easy change) based authentication
for my application.

Now I click the OK button of the New ASP.NET Project dialog.

I'm taken to a Configure Microsoft Azure Web App dialog. This is for my application's later hosting on the Web. I'll just click the Cancel button since I want to configure that later – or never in case I deploy my application elsewhere.

That's it for now: my application is ready. In order to run it inside my browser, I'll select Debug / Start Debugging from the menu, or use the F5 shortcut:

When I do this, Visual Studio starts a local Web server (IIS Express), runs my browser and points it to the URL of my site on that server, and finally attaches to the running code in debug mode so that it can catch any exception or show the code when I read a breakpoint.

This is what I get in my browser:

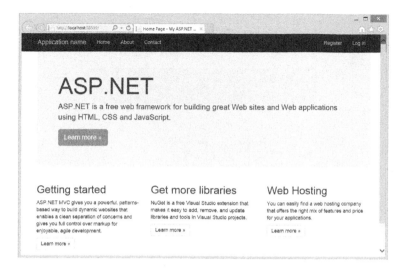

What's nice is that the site is responsive (the default template uses Boostrap):

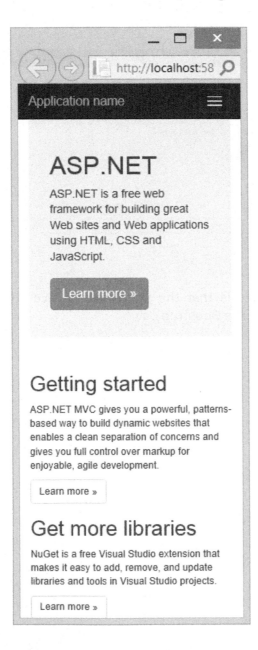

That application also has a menu above, with links that take me to almost empty "About" and "Contact" pages. Also note that we already have fully-functional "Log in" and "Register" links for user authentication. If I use them, a local SQL Server database will be created and used for storage.

Well, we have kind of a nice startup after just a few clicks. Now let's see some theory before we can extend our application. Don't worry, I'll keep it short: this book focuses on getting you up and running quickly.

2. ASP.NET MVC inner workings

2.1 Principles

When our browser queries an ASP.NET MVC URL, there are three elements that work together in order to produce an HTML page:

- A *View* produces the HTML;
- A *Controller*:
    - fetches the data and provides it to the view
    - selects the view
- A *Route* selects the controller.

That's an easy process. Here's a schema of it:

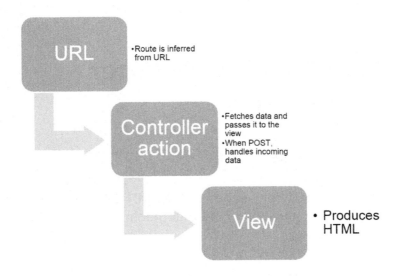

2.2 View

Once inferred from the URL, the view is looked for into the following paths:

- Views/[Controller]/[Action].aspx
- Views/[Controller]/[Action].cshtml
- Views/Shared

When coding the view, you can choose between one of two syntaxes (or add another one):

- ASPX
- Razor

We'll use Razor since it's a concise view language crafted specifically for ASP.NET MVC. ASPX is a syntax that will sound familiar to those coming from ASP.NET Web Forms.

Before we begin learning about the Razor syntax, we're going to have a look at what's part of the Visual Studio template that was created.

Let's take a look at the project structure. For this I'll use the Solution Explorer.

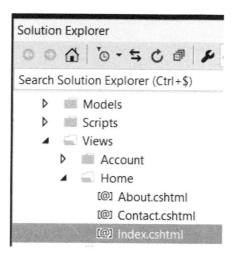

You can see that there is a "Views" folder containing a "Home" sub-folder, inside of which there is an "Index.cshtml" file. As seen above, when ASP.NET looks for the view corresponding to the "Index" action of the "Home" controller, it will get that `Views\Home\Index.cshtml` file. Sound abrupt? Bear with me.

Let's open the `Views\Home\Index.cshtml` file. Apart for the first 3 lines, it contains pure HTML markup. That's the markup that will be rendered to the browser. And it is also Razor code.

So you just learned a secret: Razor code is basically HTML code. In fact, it's HTML in which we'll add some special statements using the @ mark. Yeah, I know you're beginning to love ASP.NET MVC, or at least Razor.

Inside the solution, we can also find a `Controllers\HomeController.cs` file:

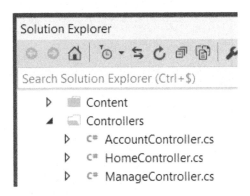

Let's open that file.

```
public class HomeController : Controller
{
    public ActionResult Index()
    {
        return View();
    }

    // ...
}
```

You can see that the class is named HomeController, and it contains a public method named Index. When ASP.NET looks for the view corresponding to the "Index" action of the "Home" controller, it will get this method.

The "Index" method contains a simple return View(); statement. It means that the default view should be returned for that action.

We're almost there. Now let's have a look at the App_-Start\RouteConfig.cs file. It contains the following code:

```
routes.MapRoute(
    name: "Default",
    url: "{controller}/{action}/{id}",
    defaults: new { controller = "Home", action = "In\
dex", id = UrlParameter.Optional }
);
```

This is the routing configuration. See the url property? It states how ASP.NET MVC will parse incoming URLs. As of now this is the only line, but you may add as many as you wish here.

What `url: "{controller}/{action}/{id}"` means is that if someone types the `http://mysite/home/index` URL in their browser ASP.NET will invoke the `Index` action from the `Home` controller. It also states that if someone types the `http://mysite` URL in their browser ASP.NET will invoke the `Index` action from the `Home` controller because they are the defaults.

Got it? Now let's sum up what happens for a sample request:

1. Someone types `http://mysite/home/index` in their browser.
2. ASP.NET MVC understands it has to look for the `Index` action from the `Home` controller, so it invokes the `Index` method from the `HomeController` class.
3. The `return View();` statement means the ASP.NET needs to return the default view.
4. ASP.NET fetches the `Views\Home\Index.cshtml` file and renders it to the browser. It's HTML which can be enhanced using the Razor syntax.

Easy, isn't it? Well that's almost all there is to ASP.NET MVC. Read those four steps again until you get them right, because they are the backbone of the ASP.NET process.

Time to put in practice all of that stuff you just learned. And I bet your fingers are itchy for coding.

3. Create an application and modify the home page

Do-it-yourself time! You should do the following two exercises. If having a hard time, you can look at the detailed steps in the do-it-yourself cheat sheet at the end of this book, but I'm sure you won't need it.

3.1 Do-it-yourself 1 - Create the application

Create a new ASP.NET MVC application project. Ensure that authentication will be done using accounts from a database (that's the default option).

Step-by-step solution at the end of this book

16   Create an application and modify the home page

3.2 Do-it-yourself 2 - Change the home page

 Change the home page so that it displays a welcome message and a "Startup" section. As a result it should look like the following:

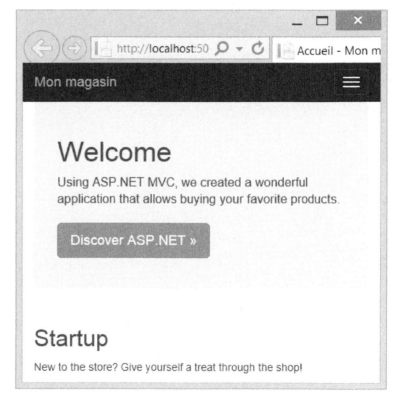

Step-by-step solution at the end of this book

4. Razor

4.1 Razor syntax

While ASPX uses the older ASP.NET Web Forms, with opening and closing tags, Razor offers a minimalistic syntax. Let's compare them:

No closing tags when they can be guessed.

ASPX

```
<div>Hello <%= userName %>, check your <a href="/emai\
l?id=<%= userId %>">e-mail</div>
```

Razor

```
<div>Hello @userName, check your <a href="/email?id=@\
userId">e-mail</div>
```

HTML and C# blend smoothly

ASPX

```
<ul>
  <% foreach (var product in Model) { %>
    <li><%=product.Name%></li>
  <% } %>
</ul>
```

Razor

```
<ul>
  @foreach (var product in Model) {
    <li>@product.Name</li>
  }
</ul>
```

Conditions

End of instructions are implicit in Razor. Notice there is no closing @.

```
<div>
  <h1>Welcome</h1>
  @if(User.Indentity.IsAuthenticated) {
    <div>You are @User.Identity.Name, hello!</div>
  }
  else {
    <div>Please <a href="...">log-in</a></div>
  }
</div>
```

Multiline code

Use @{ ... } when your code is multiline.

```
@{
  var isAutenticated = User.Indentity.IsAuthenticated;
  var userName = User.Identity.Name;
}
<div>
  <h1>Welcome</h1>
  @if(isAuthenticated) {
    <div>You are @userName, hello!</div>
  }
  else {
    <div>Please <a href="...">log-in</a></div>
  }
</div>
```

You can place any block of C# code in your view using that syntax. You might as well fetch your whole data from a database or API in such a block, apply functional logic, and create your whole application like that. Which means you might close that book and shout "I know ASP.NET MVC !". I don't recommend you to do so, though: doing so mixes code and presentation, plus it makes the view responsible for fetching its data and applying funcional logic. Which goes again SOC (Separation of concerns). Keep reading on, and you'll make the difference between a hobby programmer and a professional one.

Do-it-yourself 3 - Add code to the home page

Display the next delivery schedule on the home page. It should be tomorrow at 9 am. Make sure the date is explicitly displayed.

The resulting page should look like the following:

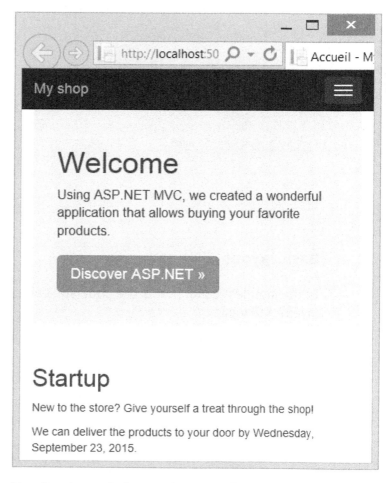

Step-by-step solution at the end of this book

4.2 Layout views

Many times you want the same HTML tags to appear on every page of your application. Instead of repeating it, you can simply refer to a layout view from your view.

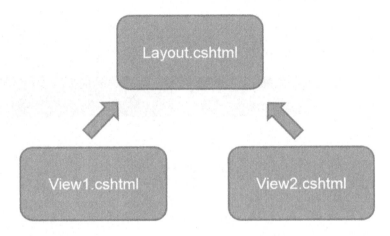

Basic layout

In the simplest case, here's the code you can use in your layout and view:

```
<html>
  <head>...</head>
  <body>
    <div class="content">
      @RenderBody()
    </div>
  </body>
</html>
```

{title:View.cshtml) @{ Layout = "Layout.cshtml"; } <p>This message will go in the "RenderBody" part of the layout.</p>

The layout is never rendered directly from an action. Instead, an action may return View.cshtml. As you can see, View.cshtml refers to Layout.cshtml. That's how ASP.NET knows that it should merge your view in its layout.

In the Layout.cshtml file, there is a RenderBody statement. It tells ASP.NET to insert here all of the content of the view that is not part of a *section*. We have no section defined in our view, so our whole view is rendered where the RenderBody statement appears.

I know you wonder what sections are. We're going to see them in a few minutes. Just to be clear, the HTML that will be rendered by ASP.NET when View.cshtml needs to be rendered will be the following:

```
<html>
  <head> ... </head>
  <body>
    <div class="content">
      <p>This message will go in the "RenderBody" par\
t of the layout.</p>
    </div>
  </body>
</html>
```

Alright, as you can see Razor's layout system is dead-easy. Let's see some more.

Layout using sections

In most cases though, you want disparate chunks of your pages to be common, not just the header and footer. That's when you use sections. Sections allows for a layout to specify which parts may be customized by a view, marking them optional as needed.

Consider the following example layout and view:

```html
<html>
  <head>...</head>
  <body>
    <div class="header">
      @RenderSection("top", optional:true)
    </div>
    <div class="content">
      @RenderBody()
    </div>
    <div class="footer">
      @RenderSection("bottom", optional:true)
    </div>
  </body>
</html>
```

{title:View.cshtml) @{ Layout = "Layout.cshtml"; } <p>This message will go in the "RenderBody" part of the layout.</p>

```
@section top {
  <h1>Some title</h1>
}

@section footer {
  <p>Copyright us</p>
}
```

Now guess what the final rendered HTML will look like?

```
<html>
  <head>...</head>
  <body>
    <div class="header">
      <h1>Some title</h1>
    </div>
    <div class="content">
        <p>This message will go in the "RenderBody" par\
t of the layout.</p>
    </div>
    <div class="footer">
      <p>Copyright us</p>
    </div>
  </body>
</html>
```

Note that the `optional: true` statements allows for a view not to include a specific section. In our example, `View.cshtml` might as well have missed a `@section top` and this section would have been empty. In case your layout states `optional: false` and that section is missing from the view, rendering the view will result in an exception.

Location of the layout

When ASP.NET MVC looks for a view or layout, it looks in the `Views\Shared` folder as we saw earlier. Since a layout is a shared file, best practice is to place it in the `Views\Shared` folder. As a matter of fact, if you look in that folder in your solution, you'll find a `_Layout.cshtml` file that is your common layout.

DRY

You know that a best coding practice is *DRY* or *Do not Repeat Yourself*. That's what layouts are about. But why would we include the following lines at the top of most of our views?

```
@{
    Layout = "Layout.cshtml";
}
```

In fact, if you look at your `Views\Home\Index.cshml` you'll see it doesn't include such a statement, though it does use `Views\Shared\_Layout.cshtml` for final rendering.

There's no magic in that. If you look again it your `Views` folder, you'll see there's a `_ViewStart.cshtml`. ASP.NET MVC automatically applies any `_ViewStart.cshtml` file to all of the views inside its folder and subfolders. Since we have a `Views\_ViewStart.cshtml` file, it will apply to all of our views. IF we open that file, we can see that it contains the following code:

```
@{
    Layout = "~/Views/Shared/_Layout.cshtml";
}
```

Bingo! That's why every view will use `Shared/_Layout.cshtml` as a layout. Of course, if you want another layout for a particular view, you can set the Layout property to another value, or event *null* in case you want no layout.

Any property set in a view will override the ones set in
_Layout.cshtml.

Good, now you know where most files of an ASP.NET MVC
project are located. Time to check your skills with some
practice.

4.3 Do-it-yourself 4 - Remove some links

 Currently, your home page and all of the
pages contain links to "About" and "Contact" views in their header menu. Remove
those two links.

Step-by-step solution at the end of this book

4.4 Helpers

In C#, when you need to factorize similar pieces of code
that have small variations, you can write parameterized
methods. Well we have just that in Razor, and they are
called *helpers*. Helpers are called like methods - that is,
with parameters, and produce HTML.

We'll see later in this book how to create your own writers
(see here) using C# or the Razor syntax itself. For now,
it'll be enough to know that ASP.NET MVC offers ready-
to-use helpers.

Here are some of the helpers readily available:

```
@Url.Content("~/relativePath/willBeConverted.jpg")
```

This one will generate an absolute URL, whatever the base URL of your application. A typical use could be for an image or link URL:

```
<img src='@Url.Content("~/relativePath/willBeConverte\
d.jpg")' />
```

And here's one that will generate a one-choice list using any IEnumerable<T> collection you provide it. Its overrides are flexible, so you may provide it with a simple array of strings as well as a LINQ query result with custom classes.

```
@Html.ListBox("name", enumerableList)
```

A very common one, to, used to generate a link (the <a/> HTML element) to one of your actions:

```
@Html.Action(label, actionName, controllerName)
```

What's neat about it is that you don't reference a path. Which means that if your routes change (e.g. for SEO purposes), you won't need to change any Html.Action parameters.

As stated earlier, since Razor allows you to place any block of code in a view using the @{ ... } syntax, you might think you are ready to code your application. However, there are many things you may want to do for a view to render:

- Taking into account any HTTP POST values coming from a form.
- Manage connection to data sources (databases, APIs and the like).
- Apply functional logic

ASP.NET MVC allows you to do all of this in a neat, separated way. So please refrain yourself from coding all of this in your view, and read on. Let's learn how to do this in a professional way.

5. Understanding ASP.NET MVC

5.1 Flashback

A quick reminder about the ASP.NET MVC process before we move on:

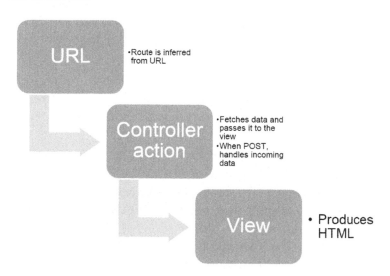

You already saw that schema before, but it should make more sense now that you saw what a route, a controller and a view are. We're going to dive deeper on those concepts, and apply them to creating our application in a professional way.

5.2 Routing

As we saw earlier, a routing engine is in charge of parsing the incoming request's URL and infering which controller and action to invoke. Practically, an action is a method inside a class (the controller).

There is no magic. You may know that ASP.NET uses the Global.asax file at the root of your web site as the default handler. Which means it will invoke its Application_Start method when your application starts. Surprise, what do we see in the Global.asax.cs file? This:

```
public class MvcApplication : System.Web.HttpApplicat\
ion
{
    protected void Application_Start()
    {
        AreaRegistration.RegisterAllAreas();
        FilterConfig.RegisterGlobalFilters(GlobalFilt\
ers.Filters);
        RouteConfig.RegisterRoutes(RouteTable.Routes);
        BundleConfig.RegisterBundles(BundleTable.Bund\
les);
    }
}
```

So basically the default templates invokes static methods on 4 classes defined in the App_Start folder. There is no magic: those methods are invoked only because they appear here, not because they are placed in the App_Start folder.

What interests us here is that line:

RouteConfig.RegisterRoutes(RouteTable.Routes);

Let's have a look at the RouteConfig.RegisterRoutes method:

```
public class RouteConfig
{
    public static void RegisterRoutes(RouteCollection\
 routes)
    {
        routes.IgnoreRoute("{resource}.axd/{*pathInfo\
}");

        routes.MapRoute(
            name: "Default",
            url: "{controller}/{action}/{id}",
            defaults: new { controller = "Home", acti\
on = "Index", id = UrlParameter.Optional }
        );
    }
}
```

Sounds familiar? That's because we saw it earlier. This is the only place of code that decides how to convert an incoming URL into an action and controller.

As we saw earlier, what `url: "{controller}/{action}/{id}"` means is that if someone types the `http://mysite/home/index` URL in their browser ASP.NET will invoke the `Index` action from the `Home` controller.

Best of all is that if we change the routing configuration, we don't need to impact the remainder of our application as long as we used the `Html.Action(label, actionName, controllerName)` helper in our views (we saw that in the helpers section).

Let's suppose that we have a ShowProductDetails action in our Products controller, and an ice-cream product which was assigned and ID of 469. With the default route, it should be invoked with the following URL:

```
http://mysite/Products/ShowProductDetails/469
```

Not that great for search-engine-optimization and URL-friendliness. So we might add the following code to our RegisterRoutes method:

```
routes.MapRoute(
   name: "ProductSEO",
   url: "{name}/{id}-Details",
   defaults: new { controller = "Products", action = "\
ShowProductDetails", id = UrlParameter.Optional }
);
```

Thanks to that new route, a user can now type in the following URL:

```
http://mysite/ice-cream/469-Details
```

That's a much friendlier URL, plus my ice-cream will be better indexed by search engines when someone searches for an ice-cream since its name appears in the URL.

Even better: the `http://mysite/Products/ShowProductDetails/469` URL is also still valid since we didn't remove the default route (but we may choose to remove as we like).

5.3 Controllers

A controller's duty

A controller:

1. Handles the incoming HTTP request and provide a response.
2. Provides actions.
3. Contains the business logic (or calls to the business logic).
4. Can be unit-tested since it doesn't reference properties of a view.

Anatomy of a controller

Writing a controller is simple: each action is a public method returning an ActionResult, and actions are placed inside a public class that is named [Controller]Controller and inherits from the `System.Web.Mvc.Controller` class.

```
public class ProductsController : Controller
{
  public ActionResult Action1()
  {
    ...
  }
}
```

According to the default route, Action1 can be invoked using the following URL:

```
http://mysite/Products/Action1
```

ActionResult

A controller can return:

- a view, which produces HTML
- whatever content (JSON, image, and so on)

What you returns goes back in the HTTP response. Usually you return a view for a browser to render the HTML, but it can really be anything. When you want to return a view, the base `System.Web.Mvc.Controller` class offers a `View` method. When you call it without any parameter, it will return the default view for your action, without passing it any model (more on that later). Look at the following basic code for an action:

```
public class ProductsController : Controller
{
  public ActionResult SayHello()
  {
    return View();
  }
}
```

This instructs ASP.NET MVC to return the *SayHello* view. ASP.NET MVC will look for a that in the following locations:

- Views/Products/SayHello.aspx
- Views/Products/SayHello.cshtml
- Views/Shared/SayHello.aspx
- Views/Shared/SayHello.cshtml

> You'll be glad to hear that, like most parts of ASP.NET, this search pattern can be changed. Even better: ASP.NET MVC is highly modular and allows you to fetch a view from anywhere you like: a database or even another web server. But that's another story and you likely do not need such advanced functionality.

ActionResult can be more than a view

You surely noticed that all of our action methods specify `ActionResult` as their return type. Up to now we called the `View()` method from our base `Controller` class, which returns a `ViewResult`.

The `ViewResult` class inherits from the `ActionResult` abstract class. And may other classes do, which allows you to return a whole lot of different content for your action, not just a view. Here are some of the types derived from `ActionResult`:

- ContentResult
- EmptyResult
- FileContentResult
- FilePathResult
- FileStreamResult
- HttpNotFoundResult
- HttpUnauthorizedResult
- JavaScriptResult
- JsonResult
- PartialViewResult
- RedirectResult
- RedirectToRouteResult
- ViewResult

I won't go into an enumeration of those types, since their names almost state it all, plus the MSDN documentation is good enough as a reference. Of interest is the fact that they represent information for several parts of the HTTP response. For instance, HttpNotFoundResult means a 404 error code, while JsonResult means a 200 code, an `application/json` content type and holds the body of the

HTTP response (JSON, needless to say). Bear with me, and we'll several of those types later on.

Passing data from the Controller to the View

As you already learned, ASP.NET will invoke a controller which in most cases will return a view. Since the view produces HTML, it is very likely to contain data (formatted as HTML). We saw that a good practice is for the controller to fetch the data, so we need some way for the controller to pass data to the view. Good news: there are several ways to do this.

A first, loosely coupled and loose way to do this is to use either `ViewData` or `ViewBag`. They both are a collection (in fact, a dictionnary) of objects to pass from the controller to the view. `ViewData` and `ViewBag` only differ in the way they are accessed to.

Here's how you add data to them (in the controller):

```
ViewData["message"] = ...;
ViewBag.message = ...;
```

And here's how you fetch data from them (in the view):

```
<p>This is a message: @ViewData["message"]<p>
<p>And the same message @ViewBag.message</p>
```

Which one to use then? It simply depends on your tastes, since they offer the same functionality. It's just a syntactic difference between those twins: `ViewData` is a *dictionnary* while `ViewBag` is a dynamic object.

5.4 Be lazy

A very common task is to create an action which returns a view. Basic creation of an action is a quick task, and you'll be glad to know that Visual Studio helps us create the corresponding view in a few cliks instead of navigating the Solution Explorer and reminding of the conventions. Let me show you.

Let's say we just added `Action1` to our Products controller

```
public class ProductsController : Controller
{
  public ActionResult Action1()
  {
    ...
    return View();
  }
}
```

All we have to do is right-click on the `Action1` method. Visual Studio shows a contextual menu:

```
public class ProductsController : Controller
{
    0 references | 0 changes | 0 authors, 0 cha
    public ActionResult Action      Go To View
    {                                 Add View...
                                      Quick Actions...
        return View();                Rename...
    }
```

Select Add View from the contextual menu and you're provided with a dialog :

At this point we don't have to select the "View name", and we can keep the "template" as "Empty". Those are details we'll learn to use a bit later. We simply make sure the "Create as a partial view" checkbox is unchecked because we didn't talk about that feature yet. As far as the layout page is concerned, you already know what that means.

So let's click the Add button and let the magic happen. Visual Studio creates the view, and we're good to go. Here's the view that was created :

```
Action1.cshtml  ⌧ ✕  ProductsController.cs        RouteConfig.cs

    @{
        ViewBag.Title = "Action1";
        Layout = "~/Views/Shared/_Layout.cshtml";
    }

    <h2>Action1</h2>
```

Quite empty, but Visual Studio just saved us quite some time. 2 minutes saved for each view, multiplied by 30 views for a medium-sized project, it sums up to an hour saved. Which means less time coding and more time having fun. And I'm yet to show you even more powerful time-savers. Time to grab a drink and celebrate !

5.5 Let's go all the way

Alright, we just created an action and a view. Let me add some code to show usage of the ViewBag. Or ViewData for those who prefer, it's just a matter of taste as you know. I'm going to display on my page the list of available languages.

In my controller action, I'll fetch the data and pass it to the view. Here's the code of my completed action :

```
public ActionResult Action1()
{
    var languages = CultureInfo.GetCultures(CultureTy\
pes.SpecificCultures);
    ViewBag.LanguagesList = languages;
    return View();
}
```

Nothing complicated here. There is no LanguagesList property on the ViewBag, but the compiler will be just fine since it's declared as a dynamic object.

Let's code the view now. Again, Visual Studio is a time saver. Instead of going to the Solution Explorer and navigate to the right folder and file, all we have to do is right-click the view in our code and select "Go to view". Neat.

Here's the code for our modified view :

```
<h2>Available languages</h2>

<ul>
    @foreach (var language in ViewBag.LanguagesList)
    {
        <li>@language.EnglishName</li>
    }
</ul>
```

Which renders (hit Ctrl-F5 while in the view) in our browser as :

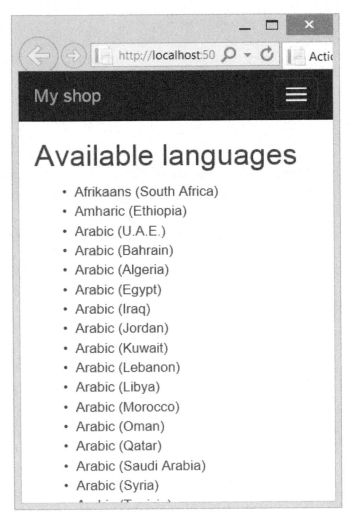

Let's just get things a bit further using a HTML helper (we saw that in the helpers section). We change the view to become :

```
@{
    var cultures = ViewBag.LanguagesList as System.Gl\
obalization.CultureInfo[];
    var listItems = cultures.Select(c => new SelectLi\
stItem() { Text = c.EnglishName });
}


<h2>Available languages</h2>

<div class="row">
    <div class="col-xs-6">
        @Html.ListBox("lang", listItems)
    </div>
    <div class="col-xs-6">
        @Html.DropDownList("lang2", listItems)
    </div>
</div>
```

Some things to note about that code :

- If you don't know why we use `div` elements like `<div class="row">` and `<div class="col-xs-6">` you might as well ignore them. They refer to Bootstrap classes used to make things look nice and have nothing to do with ASP.NET MVC.
- I'd love to avoid the first line of the C# code block and simply write `@Html.ListBox("lang", ViewBag.LanguagesList)` since that would make things simpler. Unfortunately we can't since the `ViewBag` properties are not typed and the `ListBox` method has several overloads so the runtime compiler can't infer which one

to call. Don't worry though, we're going to learn about typed models right now, which will allow us to avoid such casting code.

Here's the result :

6. Typing things up

6.1 The problem with ViewBag and ViewData

Since `ViewData` and `ViewBag` properties are not typed, using them induces several problems :

- There is no check at compile-time that a property used in the view indeed is part of the `ViewData` or `ViewBag`.
- When typing the properties in the view, there is no Intellisense help from Visual Studio: we need to type them blindly.
- Before using the properties you'll need to cast them, which makes necessary the first awful line in our untyped ViewBag example.
- If we remove or rename properties of the `ViewBag` or change the type of the objects we place in it, the view won't be aware of the change, which will result in run-time errors.

6.2 Using and typing the model

Fortunately, there's a way to get compile-time checks, Intellisense and all of the nifty things we just wished we

had: when returning a view. An action may provide it with
a model. Here's how the action passes data :

```
return View(myData);
```

Once you do this, the view will be able to access that
myData object through its Model property. But still, we
won't be nicer-off than with a ViewData or ViewBag. Easy:
since the Model can be anything, it is typed as an object.
But you can declare its type in the view using the model
directive. Let's say that we pass a MyTypes.SomeProduct to
a view. At the top of the view we may just write :

```
@model MyTypes.SomeProduct
```

Let's rewrite the preceding example using a typed model.
Our controller becomes :

```
public class ProductsController : Controller
{
    public ActionResult Action1()
    {
        CultureInfo[] languages = CultureInfo.GetCult\
ures(CultureTypes.SpecificCultures);
        return View(languages);
    }
}
```

and our view:

```
@model System.Globalization.CultureInfo[]
@{
    var listItems = Model.Select(c => new SelectListI\
tem() { Text = c.EnglishName });
}

<h2>Available languages</h2>

<div class="row">
    <div class="col-xs-6">
        @Html.ListBox("lang", listItems)
    </div>
    <div class="col-xs-6">
        @Html.DropDownList("lang2", listItems)
    </div>
</div>
```

It's a bit shorter, but most important we get :

- Intellisense support for our LINQ expression, in-cluding the selectable properties
- Compile-time check of any member from the model we use
- A cleaner code

6.3 Conventions and simplicity: introducing the ViewModel

Good things can even get better. When using a typed model, you may soon find yourself faced with other challenges :

- how do I pass several different objects to my view ?
- how do I gracefully handle a change of type in my model without ?
- how can I make sure the type of my model stated at the top of my view is correct ?
- how can I transform my data into a displayable format (e.g. the `CultureInfo[]` into a `IEnumerable<SelectListItem>`) without polluting the view or action ?

Those questions can simply be answered by creating a new class for each view: the `ViewModel`. You can name it according to the view, and it can have a property for each object you need to pass to the view.

Using a `ViewModel` is optional and pure convention. Just to make things straight we can adopt the following conventions :

- ViewModels are placed in a folder named *View-Model*, in a subfolder named after the controller that normally leads to the view (just like `.cshtml` files in the Views folder).
- For a view named *MyView*, the ViewModel would be named *MyViewViewModel*.
- The ViewModel will have a property for each user input or output the view makes.

Let's create our languages sample again from scratch using a ViewModel approach. We first create a `ViewModels` folder and a `Home` subfolder:

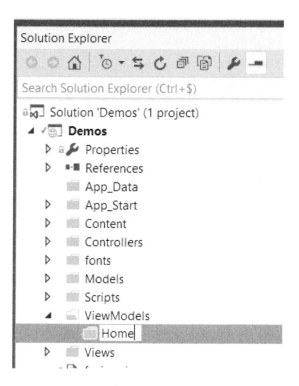

In the `ViewModels\Home\` folder we add a `ShowLanguagesView-Model.cs` file declaring the following class :

```
using System.Collections.Generic;
using System.Globalization;
using System.Linq;
using System.Web.Mvc;

namespace Demos.ViewModels.Home
{
    public class ShowLanguagesViewModel
    {
        public ShowLanguagesViewModel(CultureInfo[] c\
ultures) {
            CulturesList = cultures.Select(
                c=>new SelectListItem() { Text = c.En\
glishName }
            );
        }

        public IEnumerable<SelectListItem> CulturesLi\
st { get; private set; }
    }
}
```

As you can see, our ViewModel converts the data fetched
by the controller into displayable data. That allows for
two architectural niceties :

- the view isn't polluted with C# code
- the controller isn't polluted with presentation-re-
  lated code.

That's fine architecture. Like any architecture, it isn't strictly needed but in the long run it'll make things easier when we maintain that code over the years. Which means you could skip that ViewModel-thing if you are writing quick garbage-prone code.

Let's add a ShowLanguages action to our Home controller :

```
public class HomeController : Controller
{
    public ActionResult ShowLanguages()
    {
        var viewModel = new ViewModels.Home.ShowLangu\
agesViewModel(
            CultureInfo.GetCultures(CultureTypes.Spec\
ificCultures)
        );

        return View(viewModel);
    }
}
```

For the view creation part, let's use Visual Studio to make things easier, again. Except this time we can tell Visual Studio about our ViewModel. We right-click the ShowLan-guages action and select Add View... which pops up the "Add View" dialog. If we select Empty in the Template field we can specify a Model class, and that's where we'll type in the name of our ViewModel :

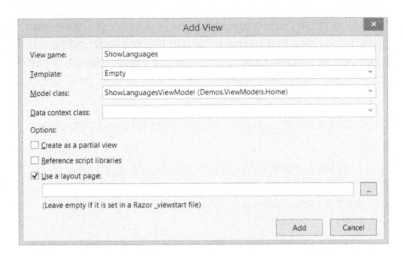

Typing in the ViewModel just ensured that the generated view has a @model directive at its top. Not that much, but it avoids any error: we get IntelliSense to help in the dialog box. That gets us an empty view :

```
@model Demos.ViewModels.Home.ShowLanguagesViewModel

@{
    ViewBag.Title = "ShowLanguages";
}

<h2>ShowLanguages</h2>
```

which we'll turn into :

```
@model Demos.ViewModels.Home.ShowLanguagesViewModel

<h2>Available languages</h2>

<div class="row">
    <div class="col-xs-6">
        @Html.ListBox("lang", Model.CulturesList)
    </div>
    <div class="col-xs-6">
        @Html.DropDownList("lang2", Model.CulturesLis\
t)
    </div>
</div>
```

Not only do we get a neat view where C# is kept to its bare minimum, but while we type we notice IntelliSense kicks in to help: no more error nor wandering around like if we used the ViewBag, plus compile-time checks:

The final result is the same as before, but we now have solid, maintainable code we can be proud of. That's professional.

 Exercise This is a small exercise that is independent from the main exercises we are doing. Just to make sure you get some practice about what we just saw.

Add a `FileSystemController` controller with an action named `Index`. The `Index` action should return a view and provide that view with a list of files in the `c:\` folder (or any folder you can give the application access to).

Create the `Index` view for the `FileSystemController` controller. That view should display the list of files in the aforementioned folder.

6.4 Entity Framework models

Being familiar with .NET, you know by now that Visual Studio and the .NET Framework are excellent productivity tools that help you build data-driven applications in no time. You'll be glad to know that Visual Studio provides good support for the Entity Framework within ASP.NET MVC.

Just in case you aren't familiar with Entity Framework, I'm going to quickly explain how to get running using Entity Framework Code First.

In the simplest scenario, we code one class for each table in a database. Let's code a Car class :

```
public class Car
{
    public int ID { get; set; }
    public string Model { get; set; }
    public double MaxSpeed { get; set; }
}
```

In order to access a database we need a *context* class. A class on which to we call methods that get and update the data from the database. Such classes are typically named *CarFactory* or *DataFactory*, or even *DataAccess*.

Easily done using Entity Framework: all we have to do is inherit from the DbContext class and add one property for each table, typed as DbSet<T>. In our example that would be :

```
public class GarageFactory : DbContext
{
    public DbSet<Car> Cars { get; set; }
    // add any other table here
}
```

We're almost there! Now we could manually create a database, but we can get Entity Framework to do this for us using pure C# code. It just takes two steps :

1. add a constructor to GarageFactory that provides an initializer
2. code the initializer.

Which gives us the following final code for GarageFactory and its initializer :

```
public class GarageFactory : DbContext
{
    public DbSet<Car> Cars { get; set; }

    public GarageFactory()
    {
        Database.SetInitializer(new GarageInitializer\
();
    }
}

public class GarageInitializer : DropCreateDatabaseIf\
ModelChanges<GarageFactory>
```

```
{
    protected override void Seed(GarageFactory contex\
t)
    {
        context.Cars.Add(new Car() { Model = "Rabbit"\
, MaxSpeed = 300 });
        context.Cars.Add(new Car() { Model = "Turtle"\
, MaxSpeed = 150 });
    }
}
```

Yes, it's that easy. Here we told Entity Framework to create the database (and clear it if necessary) whenever it doesn't exist or our model schema changes. For this we inherited the DropCreateDatabaseIfModelChanges class, and you'll be glad to know that if your needs are different you can use the following ready-made initializers :

- DropCreateDatabaseIfModelChanges
- DropCreateDatabaseAlways

... or simply create your custom one.

Now, Visual Studio can generate the necessary controller, actions and views for a full CRUD scenario in no time. We'll see that in a moment, but for now we'll manually code an action and view that display a list of cars, plus the fastest car. Though it's not necessary, we'll used a ViewModel so that we can brag about our great architecture.

Suppose we want to display the list of cars, and details about the fastest one. Let's add a ViewModel, much like the ShowLanguagesViewModel we added earlier :

```
public class CarsListViewModel
{
    public CarsListViewModel(IEnumerable<Car> cars)
    {
        CarsList = cars.Select(
            c => new SelectListItem() { Text = c.Mode\
1 }
        );
        FastestCar = cars.OrderByDescending(c => c.Ma\
xSpeed).FirstOrDefault();
    }

    public IEnumerable<SelectListItem> CarsList { get\
; private set; }
    public Car FastestCar { get; set; }
}
```

Note we compute the fastest car here, but we might as well decide to compute it in the controller.

Let's add a controller and action :

```
public class GarageController : Controller
{
    public ActionResult CarsList()
    {
        var factory = new GarageFactory();
        var viewModel = new CarsListViewModel(factory\
.Cars);
        return View();
    }
}
```

And let's finally add our view. Remember the easy way? Yes, we right-click the action, select Add View..., and fill the dialog :

It's plain easy to write the view thanks to the ViewModel and IntelliSense :

```
@model Demos.ViewModels.Garage.CarsListViewModel

<h2>All cars</h2>
@Html.ListBox("carsList", Model.CarsList)

<h2>Fastest car</h2>
<dl>
    <dt>ID</dt>
    <dd>@Model.FastestCar.ID</dd>
    <dt>Model</dt>
    <dd>@Model.FastestCar.Model</dd>
    <dt>Max speed</dt>
    <dd>@Model.FastestCar.MaxSpeed</dd>
</dl>
```

And here's the result :

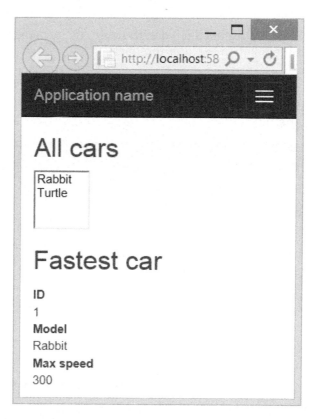

If we look into the App_Data folder, we can see that a `Demos.Models.GarageFactory.mdf` file was created. It's a local SQL Server database containing the Car table and two lines created by our `GarageInitializer` class.

> The file doesn't appear in Solution Explorer by default because it's not part of the project. In order to

> display it, we need to click the Show all files icon in the Solution Explorer toolbar.

Here's the file :

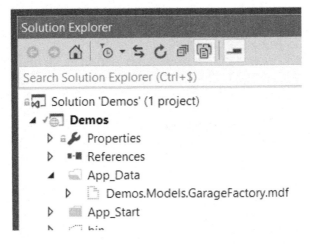

Double-clicking the file shows its structure in Server Explorer

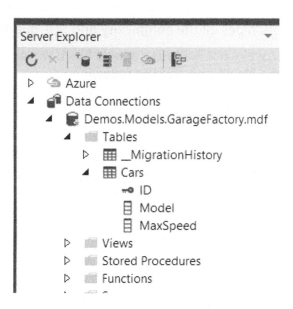

We can right-click the *Cars* table and select Show Table Data in the Server Explorer, which displays its contents :

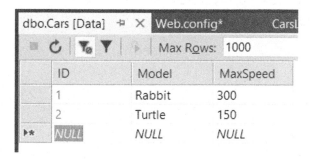

Entity Framework goes beyond the scope of this book, however it's good to note that a few lines of code have the ability of creating a database and accessing it. Entity

Framework hides all the complexity and SQL queries.

Moreover, we're not limited to a local file. If we look at the Web.config file we can see the following line :

```
<connectionStrings>
    <add name="DefaultConnection"
      connectionString="Data Source=(LocalDb)\MSSQLLoc\
alDB;AttachDbFilename=|DataDirectory|\aspnet-Demos-20\
150921061104.mdf;Initial Catalog=aspnet-Demos-2015092\
1061104;Integrated Security=True"
      providerName="System.Data.SqlClient" />
</connectionStrings>
```

When the need comes to connect to a full-size SQL Server database, all we need to do is change the connection-String. Neat.

I'm sure by now you're more than longing for some coding. Time has come.

6.5 Do-it-yourself 5 - Create the Product model and DbContext

Our Web site is an e-commerce application, meaning we need to store products. We'll store them in a database. And we'll access the database using *Code First* Entity Framework.

You must add a Product class and an Entity Framework context class.

Make sure you declare the following properties in the Product class : ID: int Name: string Description: string Price: decimal

You must also add a class named ShopFactory that inherits from the Entity Framework DbContext class, and provides access to a list of Product objects coming from the Product table of a database.

Step-by-step solution at the end of this book

6.6 Do-it-yourself 6 - Add code that creates a database with some products

 Add an initializer to the ShopFactory class you just created. The initializer must be called when the database doesn't exist or its structure changes. It must also create some products in the Product table.

Step-by-step solution at the end of this book

6.7 Do-it-yourself 7 - Display a products list

 You must modify the Home/Index view so that it displays 10 products from the database, ordered by product name.

Here's the result you should get

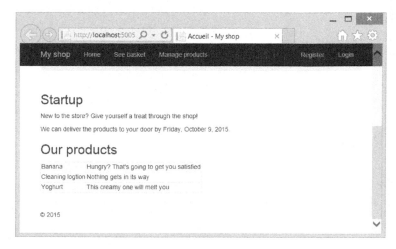

Step-by-step solution at the end of this book

7. Updating server data

7.1 Action parameters

When updating server data, you need to pass information from the browser to your application. This is simply handled by the routing system which will call your actions with parameters.

Let's look again at the default route in the Global.asax file

```
RouteTable.Routes.MapRoute(..., "{controller}/{action\
}/{id}",
    new { "...", id=UrlParameter.Optional} );
```

Note the {id} part? It means that anything coming after the action name (and separated from it by a slash sign) will be considered as an id parameter. And that this parameter is optional.

In order to get this parameter, all you have to do is add a parameter with the same name to you action method. For instance :

```
public class ProductsController : Controller
{
   public ActionResult Action1(string id)
   { ... }
}
```

Considering the default route, this action can be called simply by typing the following URL :

```
http://site/products/action1/abcd
```

In that case, our `ProductsController.Action1` method will be invoked with a value of `abcd` for its `id` parameter.

We could add as many parameters as needed to our action and modify the route accordingly. Needless to say that parameters should be short, since they add up to the URL length.

> As far as the type of the parameter is concerned (here we used `string`), ASP.NET MVC gracefully handles any conversion. So we could have declared our action with an `id` parameter of type `int` for instance. Of course, `abcd` would be rejected if we did so.

Whatever happens, we can also pass action parameters using query parameters. Consider for instance the following action :

```
public class ProductsController : Controller
{
  public ActionResult Rename(int id, string newName)
  { ... }
}
```

In order to invoke it with an id value of 15 and a newName value of sandwich, we can simply use the following URL

```
http://site/products/rename/15?name=sandwich
```

Note that sandwich is passed as a query parameter since it's not part of the route definition. We could also modify the route definition - or add a new one - in order to make it part of the URL.

7.2 Word of caution about URLs

As we saw earlier, route definitions may change later, for instance in order to improve SEO or provide user-friendly URLs. Which means it's important not to rely on them in your views.

The following view code will break if the route change, so avoid using it :

```
@* bad *@
<a href="/home/index/3">Some page</a>
```

Instead, you should prefer :

```
@* good *@
@Html.ActionLink("Some page", "Index", "Home", new { \
id=3 }, null)
```

or even :

```
@* good *@
<a href="@Url.Action("Index", "Home", new { id=3 })">\
Some page</a>
```

7.3 Do-it-yourself 8 - Display product details

You must modify the Home/Index view so a *Details* link is displayed next to each product like in the following screenshot :

Now, make sure that when the user click the *Details* link she is taken to a new *Details* view displaying the clicked product details like the following one :

Step-by-step solution at the end of this book

7.4 HTTP Post parameters

Providing action parameters through the URLs is adapted for short parameters that can appear to the user. In case you want to pass longer action parameters or hide them from the URL, you can pass them as form data. It's almost as simple.

The view should declare a form in order to have the parameters sent :

```
<form method="post">
    First Name: <input name="firstname" type="text" />
    <input type="submit" />
</form>
```

> Of course we're not limited to the POST verb. You can use other HTTP verbs when you see fit.

In order to get the parameter, all that our view needs to to is declare a parameter with the same name :

```
public class ProductsController : Controller
{
  [HttpPost]
  public ActionResult Action1(string firstname)
  { ... }
}
```

Note the [HttpPost] attribute attached to the action method. By default, an action only reacts to HTTP GET requests, that's why we need it for a HTTP POST.

Now, if you don't want ASP.NET MVC to generate part of your form, you can use an HTML helper. Our view above would become

```
@using (Html.BeginForm())
{
    <input name="firstname" type="text" />
    <input type="submit" />
}
```

The same would go for the HTML input field and submit.

7.5 Passing a full blown object

ASP.NET MVC can make your job easy when you need to update full objects. Let's suppose you created a Person class :

```
public class Person
{
    public string FirstName { get; set; }
    public string LastName { get; set; }
}
```

You can write an action that takes a Person object as a parameter

```
public class PersonController : Controller
{
  [HttpPost]
  public ActionResult CreatePerson(Person p)
  { ... }
}
```

All you need to do is to make sure that the incoming HTTP request contains parameters whose names match the properties declared in the Person class. ASP.NET will create a Person instance and pass it to your action.

For instance, we could write the following matching view:

```
@using (Html.BeginForm("CreatePerson", "Person"))
{
    <input name="firstname" type="text" />
    <input name="lastname" type="text" />
    <input type="submit" />
}
```

7.6 Sit and watch - Basic product calculator

Let's begin with a simple example. I want to create a page that allows users to compute the product of two numbers. Easy. I'll first write a ViewModel class :

```
public class ComputeProductViewModel
{
    public ComputeProductViewModel(decimal? number1, \
decimal? number2)
    {
        Number1 = number1 ?? 0;
        Number2 = number2 ?? 0;
        Result = Number1 * Number2;
    }

    public decimal Number1 { get; private set; }
    public decimal Number2 { get; private set; }
    public decimal Result { get; set; }
}
```

As seen earlier, a ViewModel can have properties for everything that is input by and output to the user.

> For such a simple example, a ViewModel is simply overkill and we could easily do without. Nonetheless I encourage you to work with ViewModels in simple cases, so that it becomes a straightforward way to

do for you. When more complex views come in your
way, you'll simply apply the same techniques and go
on seamlessly.

I'll then add a ComputeProduct action method to my Home
controller. Note that it takes two parameters: the numbers to multiply :

```
public class HomeController : Controller
{
    public ActionResult ComputeProduct(decimal? numbe\
r1, decimal? number2)
    {
        var viewModel = new ComputeProductViewModel(n\
umber1, number2);
        return View(viewModel);
    }
}
```

Now I'll right-click the ComputeProduct method and select
Add View... from the contextual menu, then select an
Empty template and my ViewModel as a model for my
view :

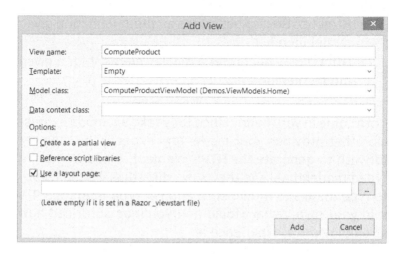

As my view code I'll type :

```
@model Demos.ViewModels.Home.ComputeProductViewModel

<h2>Product of two numbers</h2>

@using (Html.BeginForm())
{
    @Html.TextBoxFor(m => m.Number1)
    @Html.TextBoxFor(m => m.Number2)
    <input type="submit" value="Compute" />
}

<label>Result: @Html.DisplayFor(m=>m.Result)</label>
```

Not much new here, except for the use of two HTML helpers

- Html.TextBoxFor generates an input field for a given model member
- Html.Diplay generates a display element for a given model member

Both come in very handy since they take a lambda expression that provides your model and expects the member for with to generate the HTML element. Since we have a typed model thanks to the @model directive, it's plain easy to type thanks to IntelliSense and C# type-inference. Try it in your own Visual Studio and you'll be surprised how streamlined the experience is.

Let's run our view (Debug / Start Without Debugging menu). We get the following result in our browser :

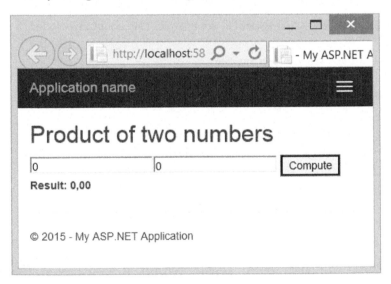

Of course, if works. When we input some numbers and click the Compute button, we get our result :

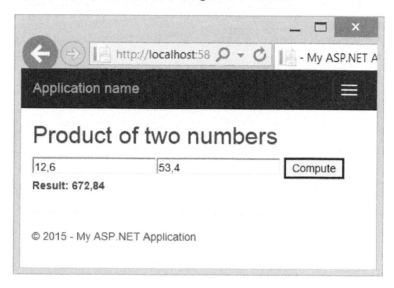

It works. No surprise. Just one more thing: remember we can provide action parameters using URL query parameters? It works here too. If we call our calculator view using the following URL :

```
http://localhost:58599/Home/ComputeProduct?number1=5.\
2&number2=8
```

...we get the following result without event clicking the Compute button (notice the URL) :

7.7 Do-it-yourself 9 - Add a search box to the products list

 You must modify the Home/Index view: add a textbox input and a button that allows the user to search products typing a part of their name. Search results must appear in the existing list, still only the top 10 ordered by name. The result looks like :

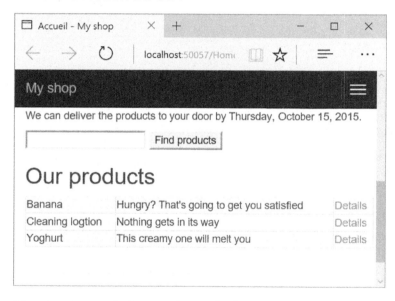

Step-by-step solution at the end of this book

8. Updating data scenario

8.1 Steps

Now we need to support data input in a real-world scenario, not just sending some partial data. When you input data in a Web application, you do so through an HTML form. In fact, that process can be broken in two steps, whatever the server-side technology

HTTP GET • User receives an input form

HTTP POST • User sends new data and receives input form populated with sent data

8.2 Controller

Those two steps mean rendering a view twice, once for HTTP GET and once for HTTP POST. Which in turn means

two actions on our controller. Your controller would typically look like :

```
public class ProductsController : Controller
{
  public ActionResult Edit(int id)
  {
    ... // fectch data from data source
  }

  [HttpPost]
  public ActionResult Edit(int id, Product p)
  {
    ... // update the data source
  }
}
```

When the data source update is successful, you probably
don't want the user to remain on the data input form.
Which means the POST action would most likely contain
a redirect statement. There is a RedirectToAction method
for this on the base Controller class. It comes in handy
since we provide the name of the action we want to
redirect to :

```
[HttpPost]
public ActionResult Edit(int id, Product p)
{
  // ...
  if(successful) {
    return RedirectToAction("Index");
  }
}
```

8.3 Automated generation of controller and views

Now is time for me to show you a gem. In case we use Entity Framework as a data access layer, Visual Studio can generate in a breeze the controller, actions and views needed for a full CRUD scenario. What's more, the generated code isn't scary and can be modified to fit your needs.

Let's see how it works. Remember we have the following model that we wrote a while ago :

```
public class Car
{
    public int ID { get; set; }
    public string Model { get; set; }
    public double MaxSpeed { get; set; }
}
public class GarageFactory : DbContext
{
    public DbSet<Car> Cars { get; set; }
    // ...
}
```

All I have to do is right-click the `Controllers` directory in `Solution Explorer` and select `Add / Controller...` from the contextual menu :

In the `Add Scaffold` dialog box I select "MVC 5 Controller with views, using Entity Framework" and click the `Add` button :

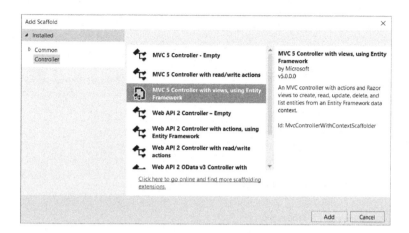

That gets me another dialog box, `Add Controller`, which I'll fill in the following way :

- Model class: `Car`
- Data context class: `GarageFactory`
- Generate views: checked (default value)

I'll leave the rest of the options to their default values. Here's the dialog box before I press the `Add` button :

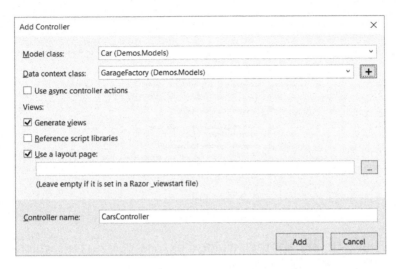

That's all there is to it! I now have full actions and views for each CRUD operation.

Let's go for instance to the list of cars. We type the `http://localhost:58599/Cars` URL in our browser and get a nice list :

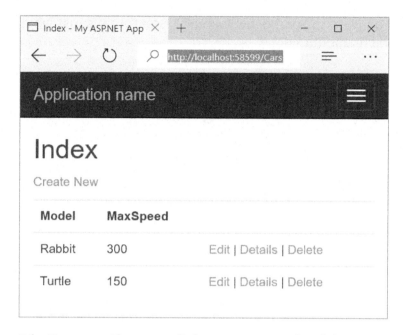

What's more, there are links to create, edit, delete and details views, all working. Time to get the paycheck and go surfing for the next week.

> Think you cannot use this wizard in real-life? Think again: if you look at the generated actions and views, they are concise and can be easily modified. Nothing is hidden from you. This is a real time-saver simply put.

Well, I can feel that your fingers are getting itchy again.

You want to try this by yourself? Great, that's just what we're about to do!

8.4 Do-it-yourself 10 - Create the products management back-office

 You must now cater for the shop products management by the shopkeepers. You are to add the necessary pages. For now, they are open for public access, but don't worry: we'll change that later. Anyway, our application isn't published yet.

Add pages that allow to :

- list all of the products from the database (and add a link to that page in the site top menu);
- add a product to the database;
- edit a product in the database;
- delete a product from a database.

Step-by-step solution at the end of this book

9. Doing more with controllers and actions

9.1 Actions can generate more than views

Since HTML is king in a Web application, we focused on the most common process where an action renders a view. However an action can generate anything that can be returned over HTTP: basically an action's output is to provide an HTTP response, and it doesn't have to be HTML.

That means our schema of a route / controller / action process has to be slightly modified. It becomes :

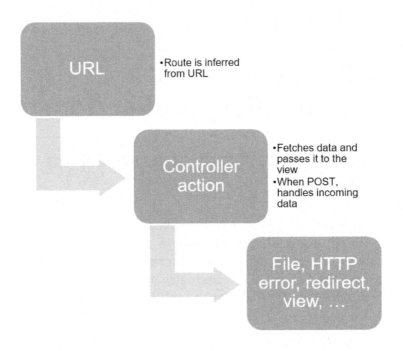

That's what the `ActionResult` class is for. When we introduced actions and their ActionResult return type we mentioned that an action can return more than a view. `ActionResult` is an abstract class from with many types derive. To name some :

- ContentResult
- EmptyResult
- FileContentResult
- FilePathResult
- FileStreamResult
- HttpNotFoundResult

- HttpUnauthorizedResult
- JavaScriptResult
- JsonResult
- PartialViewResult
- RedirectResult
- RedirectToRouteResult
- ViewResult

We already saw that we can generate a `ViewResult` by calling the `View` method from within our controller, and a `RedirectToRouteResult` calling the `RedirectToRoute` method. Following that pattern, a controller has plenty of simple methods to generate all these result types.

For instance, if we have a JPEG image contained in memory as a byte array, we can simply write :

```
public ActionResult Picture(int id)
{
  bool error = ...
  if (error)
  {
    return HttpNotFound();
  }
  byte[] image = ...
  return File(image, "image/jpeg");
}
```

The picture action could then be invoked directly by a browser or referenced from an HTML `<img />` element. For instance you could type in a view

```
<img src="@Url.Action("Picture", "Home", new { id=3 }\
)" />
```

Note that in the `Url.Action` helper, as in many helpers, you provide the parameters using an anonymous object. The `new { id=3 })` syntax allows you to pass in as many parameters as needed by the action. For instance, if my action were declared as :

```
public ActionResult Picture(int id, int width, int he\
ight)
{
  // ...
}
```

I could reference it from a view using the following syntax :

```
<img src="@Url.Action("Picture", "Home", new { id=3, \
width=100, height=50 })" />
```

9.2 Do-it-yourself 11 - Add images to the products

You must now:

- Create a folder named Images under the content folder. Add some images that represent the products you added to the database.
- Modify the home page products list: add an image next to each product description in the products list.

As a result, the home view should look like :

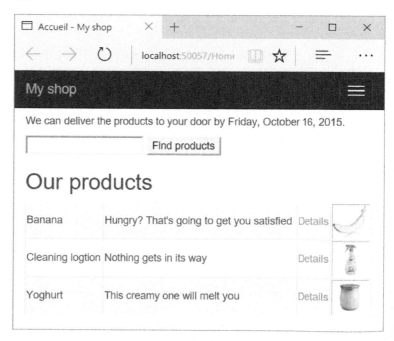

Step-by-step solution at the end of

9.3 Input validation

When writing an application, part of your work as a developper is to make sure that data entered by the user is valid before processing it. Which means meeting several criteria. If you previously worked with data validation in WPF or Silverlight, you'll be glad to hear that ASP.NET MVC relies on the same code: it supports data annotations.

With data annotations, you simply use attributes and classes from the `System.ComponentModel.DataAnnotations` namespace to mark your model classes, and presentation layers use it to validate user input and provide feedback. That means you apply a nice coding principle: DRY (don't repeat yourself).

Let's say I want to ensure that when a car is created or modified, it meets the following business rules :

- MaxSpeed cannot be less that 10 or more than 300;
- Model must not be null or empty, and it must have at least 2 characters.

I can simply annotate the `Car` class using data annotation attributes :

```
using System.ComponentModel.DataAnnotations;

public class Car
{
    public int ID { get; set; }

    [Required]
    [RegularExpression("..+")]
    public string Model { get; set; }

    [Range(10, 300)]
    public double MaxSpeed { get; set; }
}
```

This is a simple example. For advanced data validation scenarios, you'll find that the System.ComponentModel.DataAnnotations namespace offers more attributes and classes that even allow you to provide your own validation code.

Then you have to make validation work. It's quite simple actually. On the controller side, inside the [HttpPost] action (or whatever action handles user-submitted data) you check for the ModelState.IsValid property. It will be automatically populated by the ModelBinder that inject the Car parameter into your action. You code could look like that :

```
[HttpPost]
public ActionResult Create(Car car)
{
    if (ModelState.IsValid)
    {
            // code that adds car to you data source
    }

    // remain on the same view so that the user
    // sees validation messages.
    return View(car);
}
```

On the view side, there are helpers that allow you to display your error messages. Html.ValidationSummary displays a list of all the error messages for that action, and Html.ValidationMessageFor displays errors for a specific property. A view code for the Create action could look like this :

```
@using (Html.BeginForm())
{
  @Html.ValidationSummary()

  @Html.EditorFor(model => model.Model)
  @Html.ValidationMessageFor(model => model.Model)

  @Html.EditorFor(model => model.MaxSpeed)
  @Html.ValidationMessageFor(model => model.MaxSpeed)
}
```

10. Basic security

Completely securing an ASP.NET MVC application goes beyond the scope of this book. Most of it relies on techniques that are not specific of ASP.NET MVC. There are however some basic steps you can take in order to prevent common attacks.

10.1 Preventing Cross-Site Scripting

Cross-Site Scripting, or XSS, is the technique where a hacker forces a victim's browser to make a request to your application. If you cannot detect XSS, that means your application may perform actions that were initiated without a user even knowing it. Which is bad if your site is about making money transfers, for instance.

A first rule of thumb is never to modify data based on a HTTP GET request. Rely on other adequate HTTP verbs for this, like POST or UPDATE. Second, a technique is to ensure that a user makes a GET request before initiating a POST or UPDATE request. Which is easily done using an anti-forgery token.

All you have to do is inject a hidden field in the page that renders to the user using the HTTP GET request, and check that this field is the same when the POST or UPDATE request comes in afterwards. Practically there are two steps to take in your code :

1. In the view, call the `Html.AntiForgeryToken()` helper inside the form.
2. On the POST or UPDATE action, add a `ValidateAn-tiForgeryToken` attribute.

That's all there is to do. As a result, your view would look like :

```
@using (Html.BeginForm())
{
   @Html.AntiForgeryToken()
   ...
}
```

and your POST (or whatever) action :

```
[HttpPost]
[ValidateAntiForgeryToken]
public ActionResult Create(Car car)
{
   ...
}
```

10.2 Rejecting extra fields

Suppose your `Car` model has a `Price` property because this property may be read and modified from some secure part of the site. You however do not want unidentified users to change the price of a car. However, if you take a

Car object as your action parameter, nothing stops a malicious user from hand-crafting a POST request containing a Price field. If you write your action as the following code, the Price property will be updated :

```
[HttpPost]
[ValidateAntiForgeryToken]
public ActionResult Create(Car car)
{
    . . .
}
```

Not having a Property field in the view changes nothing: it's quite easy to hand-craft any POST request since it is pure text.

That's why you need to explicitly tell the ModelBinder which fields you expect in the POST request, for more security. This is done using the Bind attribute :

```
[HttpPost]
[ValidateAntiForgeryToken]
public ActionResult Create([Bind(Include = "Model,Max\
Speed")] Car car)
{
    . . .
}
```

10.3 Identifying users

ASP.NET MVC builds on top of ASP.NET which has a rich provider model. Out of the box, you get several identity providers, and will find many more. Or even code your own: it's as easy as inheriting the `MemberShip` class and overriding the `ValidateUser` method. You simply register the chosen identity provider in the application's root Web.config file.

Whatever the provider you choose, there's a unified API to access it. From whithin your actions and views you can call the `User` property. Plus you get the `Authorize` attribute. Any action that you decorate with that attribute will reject unauthenticated users. If you prefer to reject roles or specific users, the `Authorize` attribute has properties for this.

The final step is to enable authentication in your Web.config file and specify the authentication URL.

10.4 Do-it-yourself 12 - Secure the back-office

Currently, any user may access the back-office. You must ensure that

- Users can register an account
- Users can log-in
- Only the "admin@ourshop.com" user may access the back-office

Step-by-step solution at the end of this book

11. Going further

By now, you know the tools necessary to create an ASP.NET MVC application. You should be able to create your first application or site and learn by yourself.

When you are ready to progress further, this chapter gives you a few trails you may venture on.

11.1 Deploying your site

It's quite easy actually. The first part is to find some hosting: basically, that's just a machine with IIS installed and configured. As of writing this book, Azure Application Service offers free hosting from Microsoft.

The second part is to actually deploy your code. Visual Studio will guide you: just right-click your web project in the Solution Explorer and select "Publish". Then follow the wizard.

11.2 Creating Razor helpers

Helpers allow you to factorize Razor code. If you liked the ones baked into ASP.NET MVC you sure will want to create your own.

It's easy: just declare your helper in a view, using Razor code :

```
@helper Remaining(DateTime date) {
  if (date < DateTime.Now)
  {
      <div>Finished.</div>
  }
  else
  {
      <div>Within @date.Subtract(DateTime.Now).Days d\
ays.</div>
  }
}
```

Then you may use that helper in the declaring view :

```
<div>@Remaining(Model.EndDate)</div>
```

Even better: if you declare your helper in a `TimeUtils.cshtml` file in the `App_Code` folder, you may use it from any view with the following syntax :

```
<div>@TimeUtils.Remaining(Model.EndDate)</div>
```

11.3 Partial views

Partial views are declared just like standard views, and can be reused in any view. There are two helpers for injecting a partial view inside your view.

In case the view to be injected has no action, just use the `Html.Partial` helper.

If you want an action to be called and render a partial view, use the Html.Action helper. The resulting HTML will be injected inside the calling view.

11.4 Display and edit templates

Suppose you use the DisplayFor helper :

```
@Html.DisplayFor(model => model.Product)
```

It asks ASP.NET MVC to render the Product property. In case that property is a string or another simple type, ASP.NET MVC will kind of just call the object's ToString method.

But what if the Product property is a complex type, one that you defined as a ProductDetails class? Well, it also works. All you have to do is provide a display template by adding a ProductDetails.cshtml file in the Views/Shared/DisplayTemplates/ folder. That's neat, isn't it? Then you can code the ProductDetails.cshtml file just like it were a partial view. For instance, you could write :

```
@model ProductDetails

@if (Model != null)
{
    <div>Product: @Model.Name</div>
}
```

Neat, right? Best of all, you can do likewise for edit templates. Just use the `Html.EditorFor` helper, and place your
file in the `Views/Shared/EditorTemplates/` folder. That's
just the kind of nifty tricks that help me love ASP.NET
MVC. How about you?

12. What is ASP.NET MVC and why use it

This book assumes that you (or your boss) decided to use ASP.NET MVC knowing what it is. In case you do, you can safely ignore this chapter. But if you don't, read this chapter before reading the book and you'll be good to go.

12.1 What is it ?

In a nutshell, ASP.NET MVC is a technology used to create Web applications.

Web applications are used with a browser. Example of Web applications are Facebook, Google, and in fact most of the services you use. When you enter an `http://something` url in your browser, you get a Web application.

Simply put, ASP.NET MVC can be used to create a Web application like Facebook. Or a store, which is what we do in this book's exercises.

12.2 Why use it ?

In case you know .NET and need to create a Web application, using ASP.NET makes sense since you can reuse your knowledge of the .NET Framework (or .NET Core) and language abilities (like C# and VB.NET).

There are several technologies inside of ASP.NET you may consider:

- ASP.NET Web Forms: good for creating small and large Web applications when you know almost nothing to HTTP and HTML, but have experience developing client applications (for instance Windows Forms or WPF).
- ASP.NET Web Pages: good for creating small Web applications without bothering with the structure.
- ASP.NET MVC: good for creating large Web applications when you know HTTP and HTML.
- ASP.NET Web API: good for creating REST APIs.

Though you can mix all of those technologies in a single ASP.NET Web application, choosing just one is a reasonable choice. Mixing several technologies would be done when you need to maintain for instance ASP.NET Web Forms but want to add new features using ASP.NET MVC.

12.3 Competing technologies

There are many technology stacks used to create Web applications. On a technological standpoint the following stacks would for instance allow to develop applications in a way similar to ASP.NET MVC :

- Node.JS + Express
- Ruby on Rails
- Meteor

Selecting one technology or another can be debated for a while. It often boils down to beliefs or preferences, be there can be good reasons. For instance, if you know JavaScript and HTTP but nothing about .NET, you'll probably get an easier time with Node.JS + Express than with ASP.NET MVC.

Do-it-yourself Cheat Sheet

This section contains the step-by-step solutions to the do-it-yourself exercises. You normally shouldn't need it if you follow the book in order. But I know you have only a week to learn ASP.NET MVC and I don't want you to remain stuck in any exercise. So here are the steps.

Do-it-yourself 1 - Create the application - correction

1. Open Visual Studio.
2. Click the File / New / Project... menu.
3. In the New Project dialog, select the Installed tab on the left. Select Templates / Visual C# / Web on the left. In the center, select ASP.NET Web Application. Click the OK button.
4. In the New ASP.NET Project dialog, select MVC under the ASP.NET 4.5 templates. Click the Change Authentication button.
5. In the Change Authentication dialog, select Individual User Accounts. Click the OK button.
6. Back in the New ASP.NET Project dialog, click the OK button.
7. Click the Build / Build Solution menu.
8. Run the application: click the Debug / Start Debugging menu.

Do-it-yourself 2 - Change the home page - correction

1. In the Solution Explorer (on the right-hand side), open the Views folder, then the Home folder located underneath.
2. Double-click the Index.cshtml file.
3. Locate the following code:

```
<div class="col-md-4">
    <h2>Get more libraries</h2>
    ...
</div>
<div class="col-md-4">
    ...
</div>
```

1. Replace that code with the following one :

```
<div class="col-md-4">
    <h2>Startup</h2>
    <p>
        New to the store? Give yourself a treat t\
hrough the shop!
    </p>
</div>
```

Do-it-yourself 3 - Add code to the home page - correction

1. Open the `Views/Home/Index.cshtml` file.
2. Locate the following code

```
<p>
     New to the store? Give yourself a treat throu\
gh the shop!
</p>
```

1. Replace it with the following one :

```
<p>
     New to the store? Give yourself a treat throu\
gh the shop!
</p>
<p>
     We can deliver the products to your door by @\
DateTime.Now.AddDays(1).ToLongDateString().
</p>
```

Do-it-yourself 4 - Remove some links - correction

1. Open the `Views/Shared/_Layout.cshtml` file.
2. Locate and delete the following lines of code :

```
    <li>@Html.ActionLink("About", "About", "Home")</l\
i>
    <li>@Html.ActionLink("Contact", "Contact", "Home"\
)</li>
```

Do-it-yourself 5 - Create the Product model and DbContext - correction

1. In the Solution Explorer, right-click the Models folder and select Add / Class ... from the contextual menu.
2. In the Add New Item dialog box, type Product in the Name input field. Click the OK button.
3. In the Product.cs file, locate the following code :


```
class Product
{

}
```

1. Replace it with the following one :

```
public class Product
{
    public int ID { get; set; }
    public string Name { get; set; }
    public string Description { get; set; }
    public decimal Price { get; set; }
}
```

1. In the Solution Explorer, right-click the Models folder and select Add / Class ... from the contextual menu.
2. In the Add New Item dialog box, type ShopFactory in the Name input field. Click the OK button.
3. At the top of the ShopFactory.cs file, add the following using statement :

```
using System.Data.Entity;
```

1. In the ShopFactory.cs file, locate the following code :

```
class ShopFactory
{

}
```

1. Replace it with the following one :

```
public class ShopFactory : DbContext
{
    public DbSet<Product> Products { get; set; }
}
```

Do-it-yourself 6 - Add code that creates a database with some products - correction

1. At the bottom of the ShopFactory.cs file, add the following code right before the final } :

```
public class ShopInitializer : DropCreateDatabase\
IfModelChanges<ShopFactory>
    {
        protected override void Seed(ShopFactory cont\
ext)
        {
            context.Products.Add(new Product() { Name\
 = "Yoghurt", Description = "This creamy one will mel\
t you", Price=5.4M });
            context.Products.Add(new Product() { Name\
 = "Cleaning logtion", Description = "Nothing gets in\
its way", Price = 64M });
            context.Products.Add(new Product() { Name\
 = "Banana", Description = "Hungry? That's going to g\
et you satisfied", Price = 3M });
        }
    }
```

1. Add the following constructor to the ShopFactory class :

```
public ShopFactory()
{
    Database.SetInitializer(new ShopInitializer()\
);
}
```

As a result, the ShopFactory class should now look like the following:

```
public class ShopFactory : DbContext
{
    public ShopFactory()
    {
        Database.SetInitializer(new ShopInitializ\
er());
    }

    public DbSet<Product> Products { get; set; }
}
```

Do-it-yourself 7 - Display a products list - correction

1. In the Solution Explorer, open the Controllers / HomeController.cs file.
2. In the HomeController.cs file, locate the following code :

```
public ActionResult Index()
{
    return View();
}
```

1. Replace it with the following one :

```
public ActionResult Index()
{
    var factory = new ShopFactory();
    var products = factory.Products.ToList();
    return View(products);
}
```

1. In the Solution Explorer, open the Views / Home / Index.cshtml file.
2. In the Index.cshtml file, locate the following code :

```
<div class="row">
    <div class="col-md-4">
        <h2>Startup</h2>
        <p>
            New to the store? Give yourself a tre\
at through the shop!
        </p>
        <p>
            We can deliver the products to your d\
oor by @DateTime.Now.AddDays(1).ToLongDateString().
```

```
        </p>
      </div>
   </div>
```

1. Replace it with the following one :

```
   <div class="row">
      <div class="col-md-4">
         <h2>Startup</h2>
         <p>
            New to the store? Give yourself a tre\
at through the shop!
         </p>
         <p>
            We can deliver the products to your d\
oor by @DateTime.Now.AddDays(1).ToLongDateString().
         </p>
      </div>
      <div class="col-md-8">
         <h2>Our products</h2>
         <table class="table-striped table-bordere\
d table-responsive">
            @foreach (var product in Model)
            {
               <tr>
                  <td>@product.Name</td>
                  <td>@product.Description</td>
               </tr>
            }
         </table>
```

```
    </div>
  </div>
```

1. Click the Build / Build Solution menu.
2. Run the application: click the Debug / Start Debugging menu.

Do-it-yourself 8 - Display product details - correction

1. In the Solution Explorer, open the Views / Home / Index.cshtml file.
2. In the Index.cshtml file, locate the following code :

```
<td>@product.Description</td>
```

1. Replace it with the following one :

```
<td>@product.Description</td>
<td>@Html.ActionLink("Details", "Details", new { \
id = product.ID })</td>
```

1. In the Solution Explorer, open the Controllers / HomeController.cs file.
2. In the HomeController.cs file, add the following method inside the HomeController class :

```
public ActionResult Details(int id)
{
    var factory = new ShopFactory();
    var found = factory.Products.Where(p => p.ID \
== id).FirstOrDefault();
    return View(found);
}
```

1. Right-click the Details method. From the contextual menu, select Add View ....
2. In the Add View dialog, enter the following values :

- View name: Details
- Template: Details
- Model class: Product (whatever your namespace here)
- Data context class: (leave empty)

1. Click the Add button of the Add View dialog.
2. Click the Build / Build Solution menu.
3. Run the application: click the Debug / Start Debugging menu.

Do-it-yourself 9 - Add a search box to the products list - correction

1. In the Solution Explorer, open the Controllers / HomeController.cs file.
2. In the HomeController.cs file, locate the following code :

```
public ActionResult Index()
{
    var factory = new ShopFactory();
    var products = factory.Products.ToList();
    return View(products);
}
```

1. Replace it with the following one :

```
public ActionResult Index(string searchCriteria)
{
    var factory = new ShopFactory();
    IQueryable<Product> prods = factory.Products.\
OrderBy(p => p.Name);

    if (searchCriteria != null)
    {
        prods = prods.Where(p => p.Name.Contains(\
searchCriteria));
    }
    var products = prods.Take(10).ToList();
    return View(products);
}
```

1. In the Solution Explorer, open the Views / Home / Index.cshtml file.
2. In the Index.cshtml file, locate the following code :

```
<div class="col-md-8">
    <h2>Our products</h2>
```

1. Replace it with the following one :

```
<div class="col-md-8">
    @using (Html.BeginForm())
    {
        @Html.TextBox("searchCriteria")
        <input type="submit" value="Find products\
" />
    }
    <h2>Our products</h2>
```

1. Click the Build / Build Solution menu.
2. Run the application: click the Debug / Start Debugging menu.

Do-it-yourself 10 - Create the products management back-office - correction

1. Open the Views/Shared/_Layout.cshtml file.
2. Locate the following code :

```
<li>@Html.ActionLink("Home", "Index", "Home")</li>
```

1. Replace it with the following one :

```
<li>@Html.ActionLink("Home", "Index", "Home")</li>
<li>@Html.ActionLink("Manage products", "Index", \
"Products")</li>
```

1. In the Solution Explorer, right-click the `Models` folder and select `Add / Controller ...` from the contextual menu.
2. In the `Add Scaffhold` dialog, select "MVC5 Controller with views, using Entity Framework", then click the `Add` button.
3. In the `Add Controller` dialog, enter the following values :

   - Model Class: Product (whatever your namespace here)
   - Data context class: ShopFactory (whatever your namespace here)
   - Use async controller actions: unchecked
   - Generate views: checked
   - Use a layout page: checked, leave the textbox below empty
   - Controller name: ProductsController

1. Click the `Add` button of the `Add Controller` dialog.
2. Click the `Build / Build Solution` menu.
3. Run the application: click the `Debug / Start Debugging` menu.

Do-it-yourself 11 - Add images to the products - correction

1. In the Solution Explorer, right-click the Content folder and select Add / New Folder ... from the contextual menu.
2. Name the newly added folder Images.
3. Add 3 pictures. Let's suppose they are named "banana.jpg", "yogurth.jpg" and "spray.jpg"
4. In the Models\Product.cs file, inside the Product class, locate the following code :

```
public decimal Price { get; set; }
```

1. Replace it with the following one :

```
public decimal Price { get; set; }
public string ImageName { get; set; }
```

1. In the Models\Product.cs file, inside the ShopInitializer class, locate the following code :

```
    context.Products.Add(new Product() { Name = "Yogh\
urt", Description = "This creamy one will melt you", \
Price=5.4M });
    context.Products.Add(new Product() { Name = "Clea\
ning logtion", Description = "Nothing gets in its way\
", Price = 64M });
    context.Products.Add(new Product() { Name = "Bana\
na", Description = "Hungry? That's going to get you s\
atisfied", Price = 3M });
```

1. Replace it with the following one :


```
    context.Products.Add(new Product() { Name = "Yogh\
urt", Description = "This creamy one will melt you", \
Price=5.4M, ImageName="yoghurt.jpg" });
    context.Products.Add(new Product() { Name = "Clea\
ning logtion", Description = "Nothing gets in its way\
", Price = 64M, ImageName="spray.jpg" });
    context.Products.Add(new Product() { Name = "Bana\
na", Description = "Hungry? That's going to get you s\
atisfied", Price = 3M, ImageName="banana.jpg" });
```

1. In the `Controllers\HomeController.cs` file, inside the `HomeController` class, add the following method :

```
    public ActionResult Picture(int id)
    {
        var factory = new ShopFactory();
        var product = factory.Products.Where(p => p.I\
D == id).FirstOrDefault();

        if (product == null)
        {
            return HttpNotFound();
        }

        var img = new WebImage(string.Format("~/Conte\
nt/images/{0}.jpg", product.ImageName));
        img.Resize(50, 50);
        return File(img.GetBytes(), "image/jpeg");
    }
```

1. Open the Views/Home/Index.cshtml file.
2. Locate the following code

```
    <td>@Html.ActionLink("Details", "Details", new { \
id = product.ID })</td>
```

1. Replace it with the following one :

```
<td>@Html.ActionLink("Details", "Details", new { \
id = product.ID })</td>
    <td><img src='@Url.Action("Picture", new { id = p\
roduct.ID })' /></td>
```

Do-it-yourself 12 - Secure the back-office - correction

1. Open the `Controllers\HomeController.cs` file.
2. Locate the following code

```
public class ProductsController : Controller
```

1. Replace it with the following one :

```
[Authorize(Users="admin@ourshop.com")]
public class ProductsController : Controller
```

Definitions

Bootstrap

A widely used HTML framework using responsive design. Available at http://getbootstrap.com[1]

Dynamic object

A dynamic object allows you to access properties (and other members) that are interpreted at run-time. It's a quite recent addition to the C# language that allows developers to code like if they were using VB.NET with Strict=Off.

In the following example, the last line wouldn't even compile if it weren't declared as a *dynamic* :

```
dynamic maListe = new List<Person>();
maListe.Add(new Person()); // compiles and runs corre\
ctly
maListe.Add(new Dog()); // compile but throws an exce\
ption at run-time
```

---

[1]http://getbootstrap.com

Entity Framework

An ORM framework included in the .NET Framework. Other examples of ORM frameworks include nHibernate or LINQ to SQL.

Project

A project represents all the files and actions needed to build an assembly (DLL or EXE). It appears as a folder tree containing files in the Solution Explorer.

It is stored on the disk as a `csproj` (for C#) or `.vbproj` (for VB.NET) file. It's an XML file that states which action to take on each file. Which is very handy when you need to build the project in a build factory.

Solution

A concept in Visual Studio that allows grouping of several projects.

On the disk, a solution is stored in a `.sln` file that simply contains a list of relative links to the projects it's made of.

This means that if necessary, you can create several solutions for a same application, which may be useful for large projects.

Solution Explorer

A window that shows a view of all the files in your solution, much like Windows Explorer. By default, it should be on the right-hand side of Visual Studio. If you cannot see it, use the menu View / Solution Explorer.

A word from the author

I sincerely hope you enjoyed reading this book as much as I liked writing it and that you quickly become proficient enough with ASP.NET MVC.

This book is my first book, and you can expect me to write several more in the coming months.

If you would like to get in touch you can use :

- email: books@aweil.fr
- Facebook: https://www.facebook.com/learnaspnetmvc

In case your project needs it, I'm also available for speaking, teaching, consulting and coding. All around the world.

If you liked this book, you probably saved a lot of time thanks to it. I'd be very grateful if you took some minutes of your precious time to leave a comment on the site where you purchased this book. Thanks a ton !

CPSIA information can be obtained
at www.ICGtesting.com
Printed in the USA
LVOW04s2246020516

486385LV00012B/130/P